Komodo Dragon

Komodo Dragon

ON LOCATION

KATHY DARLING

PHOTOGRAPHS BY TARA DARLING

HOUGHTON MIFFLIN BOSTON • MORRIS PLAINS, NJ

California • Colorado • Georgia • Illinois • New Jersey • Texas

Acknowledgments

With great appreciation to Dr. Walter Auffenberg, Professor Emeritus of the University of Florida, who gave so generously of his time and shared some of his knowledge of the Komodo dragons.

Thank you to the following dragon experts at the National Zoo in Washington, D.C., for their invaluable assistance and for checking the manuscript for accuracy: Patricia Ann Jaffray, editor of the *Dragon Doings* newsletter, Dr. Dale Marcellini, Curator of Herpetology, National Zoological Park, and Trooper Walsh, Biologist, Department of Herpetology, National Zoological Park.

The National Zoo is responsible for the first successful captive breeding program of dragons outside Indonesia. They are instrumental in promoting dragon conservation worldwide. A substantial donation has been made by the Publisher to the Komodo Dragon Trust Fund to help further their work.

Komodo Dragon: On Location, by Kathy Darling, photographs by Tara Darling.

Reprinted by arrangement with William Morrow & Company.

Houghton Mifflin Edition, 2001

Printed in the U.S.A.

ISBN: 0-618-05977-6

123456789-B-06 05 04 03 02 01 00

Contents

Komodo dragons are good swimmers. They regularly swim to neighboring islands in search of food.

1 Dragon Island

Komodo Island is a dangerous place. There are more deadly snakes, scorpions, and poisonous spiders here than anywhere else in the world. Earthquakes shake the land. Huge tidal waves crash against the shores. Volcanoes on neighboring islands blast smoke and ash into the air, smothering all the plants and animals.

Even the waters around Komodo are hazardous. There are swift currents, whirlpools, and man-eating sharks. For hundreds of years a tribe of pirates called "boogeymen" attacked ships that sailed by.

These are all scary things, but to some people, there's something even more frightening about Komodo: the giant meat-eating lizards that live there. Early explorers called them dragons and warned other travelers of the danger by writing **Beware! Here Be Dragons!** on maps of the island.

Not many people really believed there were dragons on Komodo. But just in case, they stayed away. No one had much reason to go there. Komodo lies in the middle of Indonesia, a nation of 17,000 islands that form a barrier between the Pacific and Indian oceans. It is a small island, just twenty-two miles long and twelve miles wide, with not much flat land on which to raise crops.

Storybook dragons are probably based on descriptions of giant reptiles such as the Komodo lizards. In fairy tales dragons can do remarkable things. They can fly and even breathe fire. But as in stories about

Dragons can't suck because they have no diaphragm, and their slender tongues are no good for lapping. They drink by lifting their heads and letting water run down their throats.

other big, scary animals, facts are wildly exaggerated. A lot of fiction has been added to a little bit of fact. People have even combined accounts about several different animals to create a scary monster—the dragon that exists only in fairy tales.

My daughter Tara and I love dragon stories, both the fairy-tale ones and the true science ones. But we think they should be kept separate. Since it is the job of scientists to separate fact from fiction, we decided to go to Komodo Island and gather facts so we could write a book about dragons that would be 100 percent true. Our friends thought we were crazy to go to such a scary place. I guess we are crazy—about dragons!

Komodo is close to the equator. As you would expect in a tropical place, it is always hot. Sometimes it is hot and wet: From December through March the monsoon winds bring heavy rains. The rest of the year it is hot and dry: From April to November almost no rain falls on Komodo Island and wildfires threaten everything that lives there.

It was July when we got our first view of the island. As our boat chugged toward the dock, we could see that the riverbeds were empty. The waist-high grass on the jagged peaks was yellow and dry. The only things that looked alive were skinny palm trees sticking above the grass like green lollipops.

Komodo is a national park, and we needed to check in at the rangers' office.

The dragon that chased Tara was a young one, about five feet long. Just how big can they grow? No one knows, but dragons continue to grow in spurts throughout their lives.

From the beach we could see it, a wooden building on stilts. So we headed over to show the papers that gave us permission to study the dragons. I had just started up the steps when Tara screamed.

"Dragon!" she yelled, pointing to a dark shadow lurking under the building. I turned in time to see her sprint back onto the beach. A five-foot-long dragon was chasing her. Although it wasn't moving quickly, it was gaining on her. Tara couldn't run very fast in the sand, especially since she was wearing a backpack with fifty pounds of camera equipment in it. Then, suddenly, the chase was over. The dragon stopped to eat a dead fish that had washed up onto the sand. Apparently Tara hadn't been its target after all. We both breathed a sigh of relief.

Dragons don't usually eat humans. That's because there have not been many people on Komodo. The island was uninhabited until the sultan of nearby Sumbawa sent criminals there in the 1800s. It was the worst punishment he could think of. Today, a few fishermen live on Komodo in a small village that is close to the ranger station. *Oras,* as the native people call the dragons, have eaten a few of these villagers. And now that dragons have become more popular with tourists, maybe tourists will become more popular with dragons.

Komodo dragons have not been well studied. Maybe it's because they are so big and dangerous. It could be because they are reptiles. Many people have a fear of reptiles, perhaps inherited from ancestors who lived in the path of poisonous snakes and giant crocodiles.

There is still a lot to learn, and work for many young scientists in the years to come. If you are brave enough to follow the dragon to its lair, maybe you will be the one to discover something new.

The dragon's lair is a shallow den, which it makes by burrowing into the ground. The adult dragon sleeps curled up in this earth burrow to keep from getting too cold at night.

2 In Cold Blood

The dragon that lives in your imagination is probably very much like the dragon lizards of Komodo—big, powerful, dangerous reptiles that rule their world.

Reptiles, a class of animals with over 6,000 species, include turtles, crocodiles and alligators, the tuatara, snakes, and lizards. More than half the reptiles are lizards. Most of those are small. Only half a dozen species grow more than six feet in length. All of these big lizards are monitors, or varanids as they are called by scientists. The Komodo dragon, *Varanus komodoensis,* is the biggest of them all. Dragons are thought to live fifty years or more and unlike most mammals, birds, and fishes, these reptiles continue to grow throughout their lives. Some scientists think that the monitor lizards of Komodo are capable of reaching eleven feet in length.

Humans have five senses: touch, sight, hearing, smell, and taste. Dragons have all these, but they aren't organized the way ours are. The oras also gather information about the world around them with an amazing sixth sense. Here's how their senses are the same as ours and how they differ.

TOUCH: Dragons come covered in body armor. The hard, lumpy bumps are called scales. With a skin made of scales, some reinforced with bone, it is difficult to feel anything. So dragon scales have special spots that are sensitive to touch. These sensory plaques are connected directly to nerves; every scale has at least one plaque.

A dragon's scaly skin is made of keratin, the same material as your fingernails.

Dragons are smart lizards, but even in the biggest ones, the brain is only one and a half inches long and a half inch wide.

The scales around the ears and on the lips, chin, and bottom of the feet each have three, four, or more sensory plaques.

SIGHT: The big, brown eyes of a dragon have round pupils, more like the eyes of mammals than those of many of their reptile relatives. They have good vision and the images they see are in color. It is thought that the dragon's vision is much like ours.

HEARING: Dragons have very visible earholes but sometimes act as though they are deaf. They actually can hear quite well. Probably they don't respond to most sounds because they are just not interested in them.

SMELL: You can see the nostrils on the end of a dragon's snout. Monitors can smell through their noses but this sense doesn't work as well as ours. Lizards don't have a diaphragm, the muscle that pushes air in and out of our lungs. Since a dragon cannot draw air into its nose, it can't get very much information that way unless a breeze is blowing directly into its nostrils or an object is only a few feet away.

TASTE: Dragons are tasteless! There are no taste buds in its mouth, none on its tongue, and only a few way back in the throat. However, if the definition of taste is the ability to recognize the flavor of items in the mouth, then dragons can indeed taste. The identification is not made by the taste buds but by an organ on the roof of the mouth that does a similar job.

THE "SIXTH SENSE": This sense, commonly called vomero-nasal, is a sort of combination of smell and taste. The dragon's specialized forked tongue gathers chemical information from the air and from the surfaces of objects. As the tongue is withdrawn into its sheath, these chemicals rub off onto pads on the floor of the mouth. The pads are pressed against two pits on the roof of the mouth that contain a little organ that translates the chemicals into information that the brain can analyze.

A notch at the front of the lower jaw

When you see a dragon's yellow tongue flicking in and out, it is easy to understand how rumors that dragons breathe fire might have started.

allows dragons to flick their tongues in and out without opening their mouths. How far they stick the tongue out and how long they keep it there depends on what they are investigating. Something of interest that is far away requires a long, slow flick in order to pick up enough particles to be analyzed. A nearby object needs only a quick flick. If the tongue actually touches an object, the amount of information increases enormously.

Sometimes people call reptiles "cold blooded." This is not a good way to describe them. The temperature of a Komodo dragon's blood is just about the same as yours. You keep your blood and your body warm by burning energy you get from food. Dragons and other reptiles can also use food energy, but they heat their bodies with the warmth of the sun whenever possible. However, overheating is more of a danger on tropical Komodo Island. Dragons, in their armored skin, can't sweat to keep cool. All they can do is pant like a dog. By moving in and out of the sun, dragons can usually keep their bodies comfortable. It is a good method of temperature control because it is so energy efficient. It enables the so-called cold-blooded animals to live where mammals and birds can't find enough food to keep warm.

107 °F is the maximum temperature that a dragon can endure. On Komodo the temperature is sometimes higher than that, even in the shade. An overheated ora tries to find a burrow, but in emergencies, it can cool down quickly by panting like a dog.

With one exception, all monitor lizards are carnivorous: They eat meat.

3 Snack Attack

Don't look for a photograph of a dragon flashing its deadly teeth. You won't find one here or anywhere else. The flesh-shredding teeth that everyone fears are almost completely covered by thick, spongy gums.

Even if you could see a dragon's teeth, you probably wouldn't be impressed by their size. They are less than an inch long. This is a case where size isn't important. It's design that counts. Dragon teeth, which look like those of a shark or meat-eating dinosaur, are perfect meat slicers. Like sharks, dragons can replace their teeth if they get knocked out. They are regular tooth factories, replacing an entire set every three or four months throughout their lives.

As a dragon feeds, food pushes the gums back and exposes the cleverly designed teeth. The delicate gums bleed and the blood mixes with the dragon's thick saliva, so it appears to have red spit.

Gobs and gobs of the thick spit are produced to help large chunks of food slide down the dragon's throat. Since all of its teeth are cutting teeth, a dragon can't chew its food. But it can open its mouth wide enough to swallow an entire goat, a whole hog, or half a deer in one gulp.

If the food is large, it takes time to work it to the stomach. It may take fifteen or twenty minutes to swallow a whole goat. It is difficult to breathe with a goat stuck in your throat. The dragon's solution to this problem is very clever. At the base of its tongue is a tube that goes directly to the

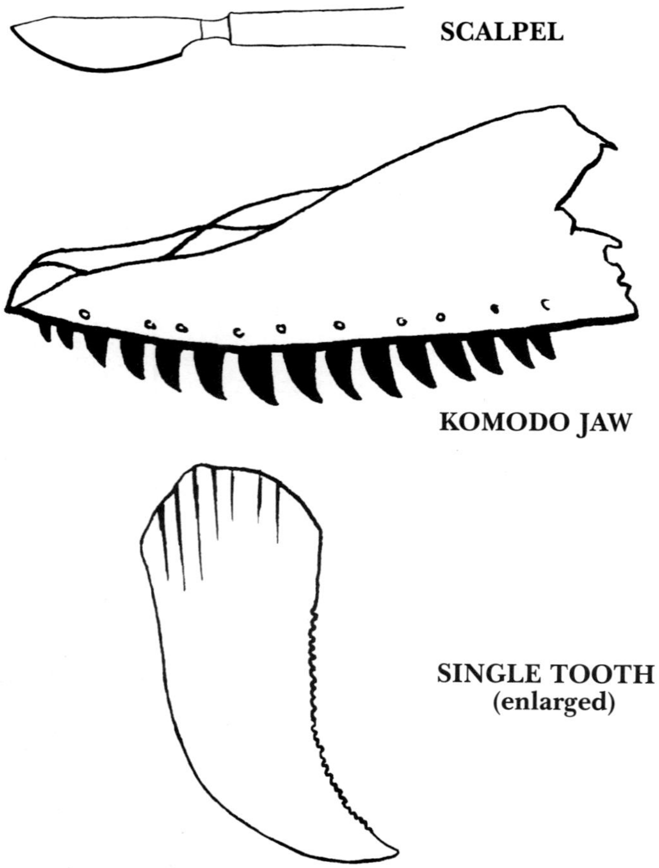

Every dragon tooth, notched like a saw on the back edge, is angled so that it cuts deeper than the tooth in front of it. All of the teeth are the same triangular shape, but those in the front and rear of the mouth are shorter than those in the middle, forming a gentle curve. This shape is so good at cutting flesh that it is used for surgeons' scalpels.

Charlotte Hommey

lungs. To avoid choking while it is eating, the dragon sticks the tube out the front of its mouth like a little snorkel. You can sometimes see it poking out the notch in its lower jaw.

The monitor has strong stomach acid to digest its food. However, a few things are not digestible. The dragon, an energy-efficient animal, doesn't waste its energy by passing these indigestible items through its body. It coughs them up in much the same way a cat gets rid of a furball. The mass of horns, hair, and teeth it expels is called a gastric pellet.

Gastric pellets are covered in vile-smelling mucus. Zookeepers have been slimed by these rancid rockets, and even dragons can't stand them. After coughing up a gastric pellet, a dragon always rubs its face in the dirt or on bushes to get rid of the mucus.

If you think of oras as bloodthirsty beasts with a never-ending appetite, you are in for a surprise. Theirs is a feast-or-

Between its sharp teeth and deadly drool, a dragon's bite is double trouble.

famine life. Big dragons eat only about twelve meals a year. Compare that with the 1,000 you eat. A lot of food is not necessary because oras are so good at using what they eat that they can live on ten percent of the food it would take to keep similar-sized mammals operating. "Waste not, want not" could be the dragons' motto. They make use of every bit of food. When they are done eating, there is nothing left but a bloodstain on the ground.

After a "snack attack" a Komodo dragon might have so much food in its stomach that its belly drags on the ground. The meals may be few in number, but they can be awesome in size. Dragons can pack away an incredible amount of meat in a single meal—as much as eighty percent of their before-dinner weight.

It takes a dragon several weeks to digest a big meal. As soon as it is finished eating, the reptile drags itself to a sunny spot to bask. Without the sun's energy to help speed up digestion, food would rot in the stomach and poison the dragon.

4 Hide and Seek

When the sun begins to heat the mountain meadows, deer come down the hills to rest in the shade of the river forests. They walk slowly, in single file, on the steep trails that wind through the tall, dry grass. It is very hot, and they are eager to reach the cool of the trees.

Still, the lead buck walks slowly, stopping often to sniff the breeze for signs of danger. He is nervous because the wind is not bringing him information about what lies ahead—such as the dragon hiding beside the narrow path.

Komodo dragons are very smart lizards, the Einsteins of the reptile world. This one has chosen a great ambush spot. It remembers that it has caught food here in the past and is now waiting patiently for "seconds."

Earlier in the morning the dragon prepared the ambush spot, trampling down the grass and scraping all the loose sticks and stones out of the attack path. As it waits, the ora's long yellow tongue constantly flicks in and out of its mouth. Suddenly, after hours of almost motionless waiting, the dragon is alert. It has caught the scent of deer.

The dragon shows no sign of excitement; it just remains crouched in its ambush spot as the overheated deer walk steadily down the path. The deer don't suspect a thing, even when they come into striking range. When the lead buck is only a few feet away, the ora springs its trap with a powerful rush. Before the four-hundred-pound deer has time to react, the dragon

This dragon is hungry. It hasn't eaten in so long that its ribs are sticking out.

Big dragons expect respect. Young ones have a special walk that signals their submission.

has knocked him to the ground. Wild-eyed with fright, the deer struggles to his feet. Before he can escape, the dragon lunges again. This time the ora gets a throat hold and begins to shake violently from side to side. The deer goes down again—this time for good—and the dragon begins to eat.

Getting food dragon style is like a deadly game of hide and seek. Although the oras have a reputation as scavengers, most of their meals are actually obtained by hunting, and the method that suits the big lizards best is hiding in ambush. Hiding increases their chances of catching an animal that can run much faster than they can (that includes just about all the animals on the island). Komodo dragons can lunge with a startlingly fast strike, but their top running speed is only about ten miles an hour. That's not fast enough to catch a deer capable of bounding along at fifty miles an hour, or a horse that can gallop at forty. Even a human can sprint faster, especially one with a dragon in hot pursuit.

Ambushes may be successful even if the prey gets away. If a dragon manages to wound something, there is still an excellent chance of getting it for a meal. Very few animals can survive a dragon bite. The tiniest of scratches can be fatal because a dragon's mouth is home to at least four types of germs that can cause blood poisoning. Mouth bacteria are one of the dragon's best weapons. Infection can kill a wounded animal in as little as three hours. One of the germs, the dreaded "flesh-eating bacteria," causes a stinky infection, and the dragon can track down its dying victim by smell. There is also some evidence that the saliva of the dragon contains chemicals that keep the blood from clotting so the victim will bleed to death.

The "seek" part of food gathering involves tracking, usually of dead or dying animals. Once dragons set out after food, whether it is a rat or a buffalo, it is almost impossible to shake them off the trail. They will track it down no matter how long it takes.

Dragons are not very fussy eaters. Although they prefer fresh meat, they will gobble up rotting carcasses crawling with worms and maggots. The big reptiles have even been known to dig up human corpses from the cemetery near Komodo village. Stomach acid that is strong enough to dissolve bones probably protects them from some of the disease-causing bacteria found in rotten meat. And having no taste buds undoubtedly makes it easier to eat some of the more rancid bits.

To find food, the ora uses a regular search pattern, checking likely spots in its territory every day. However, when the smell of decaying meat comes drifting on the breeze, a dragon will leave its territory.

An ora's sensitive nose and tongue can detect stinky stuff more than six miles away. Dragons from near and far gather at rotten feasts. There, monitors, which usually try to avoid each other, must shrug off their fears and stand shoulder to shoulder with other dragons, even ones much larger than themselves, if they want to share in a kill. It is a stressful situation.

Really big animals walk right up to the food. The others must find their place in the ranking system, which is mostly based on size. A little dragon has the most reason to be nervous, as it is in danger of becoming another item on the menu. Before it dares eat, a smaller adult (one that is four or five feet long) must show the larger lizards that it means no harm and knows its place.

The oras are quiet animals. They have no vocal cords. However, they do have ways to get a message across. When a dragon wants to draw attention to itself, it can make a loud, rumbling hiss. But it most often speaks with "body language."

A small dragon begs admission to a feast by walking with a slow, stiff-legged gait in a

THE BIG FIGHT

ROUND 1 Threats

ROUND 2 Shoving and pushing

circle around food which is being eaten by larger lizards. The little one keeps its mouth shut and its head down. These postures communicate humbleness and are promises that the animal making these "appeasement" gestures will wait till the larger oras have had their fill. When a small dragon finally enters the eating zone, it watches the larger dragons carefully. At the slightest sign that it is not welcome, the little one scurries away to avoid a fight.

Fighting is almost always between dragons of nearly equal size, and it is serious business, full of tail lashing, lunging, scratching, and biting. Often the dueling dragons get up on their hind legs in a reptile wrestling contest. This is not just a shoving match. Lives are at stake.

Sometimes a dragon that knows it is licked can break away and run off. Usually, a loser is forced to the ground, while the champion hisses in triumph and rakes it with its claws. If the winner kills the loser, it may eat him.

ROUND 3 A knock-down for the winner

ROUND 4 And a hasty retreat for the loser

In the dragon world, the males wear perfume.

5 Dragons in a Clutch

It's not easy for dragons to find mates. This has nothing to do with their scary looks or even their bad breath.

One of the reasons it is so hard to meet a monitor of the opposite sex is because it appears that there are at least three male dragons for every female. Scientists have not figured out why there are so many more males. They have a hard enough time figuring out which ones *are* the males.

It may sound strange, but even dragons have a hard time telling what sex another dragon is. Males and females look the same from a distance. They are the same color and shape and are about the same size. A closer examination doesn't give much more information. All the sexual organs are hidden inside the single hole, called the cloaca, at the bottom of the body.

Zookeepers try to determine the sex of Komodo dragons by looking inside their bodies with X-ray machines. The dragons, of course, have another way to identify each other. They use "perfume."

When a male dragon meets another dragon during the hot, dry days of July and August, which are the mating months on Komodo Island, he smells the other animal. Males, and only males, make the mating scent, so a sniffer knows he has found a female if there is no lizard perfume.

Another reason oras have a hard time finding mates is because they prefer to be alone. Males don't go out looking for a female or call out to attract one. How, then, do they find their mates? Simple. They meet over meat.

The only time dragons gather together is around a big food source. So when males join a feeding group in the summer, they take the opportunity to check and see if any of the other dragons are females. They do that by smelling animals of breeding size in the area where the hind leg joins the body. One of the glands that make the lizard perfume is located near here. If a male finds a female, he tries to attract her attention by scratching her back with the long claws of a front foot. The female usually protests with a loud hiss. At this point she isn't sure that the other dragon, an animal that is big and strong enough to kill her, is interested only in mating. Because the female is also dangerous, the male must be strong enough to overpower the female he has chosen or she might hurt him. Dragons normally do not let other big dragons get close to them—a wise policy in a cannibalistic species.

If the male has mating in mind, he lets the female know that this is his intention by flicking his tongue around her ear opening and rubbing his chin along her snout and neck where there are many sensory plaques.

About a month after a successful mating, the female ora is ready to lay her eggs. She chooses her nest site carefully. A sandy hillside is an ideal spot. Digging with her front feet, she clears a tunnel till only her tail and hind legs stick out. Then she turns around and backs into the hole. We were able to watch one female, and although we couldn't see what was happening inside the tunnel, we knew when she laid each egg because her whole body shook with the effort. When the pile of eggs, called a clutch, numbered about twenty, the dragon crawled out of the hole. Then she stuck her head back in and pushed dirt over the eggs. Finally, by stomping around, she collapsed the tunnel opening. The eggs were hidden. Although many females stay around the nest site for a few weeks, their duties as parents are over as soon as the

New research leads us to believe that dragons may keep the same mate for life.

clutch is laid.

The three-inch-long eggs are not hard-shelled like chicken eggs. The shells are rubbery and tough like leather. They are also elastic and expand as the lizard baby grows inside. At hatching time, the eggs are fifty percent bigger around than they were when they were laid. Everything a little lizard needs to grow is already inside the shell except for oxygen and water. These it gets through tiny holes in the shell called pores.

It takes almost as long for a dragon pup to develop as it does for a human child. For eight and a half months the little ora grows inside the egg, getting its food from the

© Jessie Cohen, National Zoological Park, Smithsonian Institution

This is the actual size of an average Komodo dragon egg. The baby, curled up inside, is eighteen inches long.

rich yolk. In April, at the end of the rainy season when there are lots of insects to eat, the baby dragon is ready to break out of its shell. The hatchling slashes its way out of the egg with a special tooth which grows on the end of its snout. This razorlike "egg tooth" falls off as soon as its job is done. The baby dragon may stick its head out of the egg immediately and breathe in fresh air, but it is exhausted. It rests, still curled in the broken shell, for many hours, sometimes even a whole day, before it has enough strength to dig out of the nest.

The four-ounce dragon pup is brightly colored. It is greenish black and white with yellow speckles that look almost like the little lizard has walked through a shower of gold dust. It has small reddish circles on its body, and alternating dark and light bands decorate its long, thin tail. These designs help hide a young dragon in the patterns of sun and shade of the trees, where it will live for the first year or two of life.

Treetops are good places for baby dragons to call home. There is plenty to eat there. Whatever diet they may have in later life, most reptiles begin as insect-eaters. Small dragons find beetles, ants, caterpillars, and lots of other bugs in their leafy nurseries. As they get bigger and stronger, their menu expands to include eggs, baby birds, and little lizards called geckoes. They are good hunters, more than doubling their weight in a year.

When they are about three feet long, young dragons begin to spend time on the ground, hunting small rodents and scavenging. Their bright colors start to fade to the dull gray of an adult. Now, in addition to growing longer, they begin to bulk up. The tail thickens, the head widens, and the stout adult shape emerges. A juvenile five-foot dragon may weigh only ten to fifteen pounds but a five-foot adult could weigh forty-five pounds. A ten-foot adult (only twice as long) could be thirty times as heavy as a five-foot juvenile.

Adult dragons sleep underground, but baby dragons sleep in holes in trees or underneath loose bark.

6 Lost in Time

Dragons are not dinosaurs. They are not descendants of dinosaurs either. Komodo dragons are ancient creatures, older than Komodo Island itself. The ancestors of modern monitor lizards walked the prehistoric land long before dinosaurs ever set foot on it. They outlasted them and tens of thousands of other species. Monitor lizards are survivors.

The forty-four species of monitor lizards live in tropical parts of Australia, Asia, and Africa, but Komodo dragons exist only in one tiny corner of the world. Dragons have been seen living on just four islands: Komodo and its neighbors—Rinja, Padar, and Flores. The area they originally roamed is not known. However, the 575 square miles of their present range is the smallest of any large carnivore.

When all members of a species live close together, the whole species is at risk. Sometimes the threat is a natural disaster. In 1984 it was fire, a big blaze that swept across the island of Padar and killed almost all the large animals. There was no food for the plant-eating animals, and those that lived through the fire soon died of starvation. After they had eaten all the dead animals, the surviving dragons became so desperate for food that they abandoned the island and swam to Rinja or Komodo. A few prey animals have returned to Padar, but the dragons have not.

The small number of animals in the species also puts the Komodo dragon at risk. It is estimated that on all the three

In 1993 UNESCO granted Komodo Island National Park Living Treasure status to protect the dragons in their native habitat. There are only about thirty adult dragons in zoos outside Indonesia.

home islands there are three to five thousand dragons. It is believed that there never were many more dragons on these islands. The current population is probably close to the maximum number that such dry places can support.

The dragons have survived many dangers, but the biggest threat to them may lie ahead. Oil and rich mineral deposits have been discovered on Komodo and Rinja islands. If drilling and mining are allowed, they could create pollution and damage the habitat that the dragons need to live.

The world is slowly recognizing how special the dragons are. In 1980 the Indonesian government made Komodo Island a national park and sent rangers to guard the dragons. A few years later, the United Nations put the dragon on the Endangered Species List to protect it from international trade.

In 1992 the National Zoo in Washington, D.C., and all dragon lovers had reason to celebrate. For the first time outside of Indonesia, a clutch of dragon eggs hatched successfully. In 1993 another clutch joined the dragon legions. In 1994 two successful hatchings brought the total number of babies up to fifty-five. Of the thirty-nine survivors, thirty-five have become ambassadors for conservation, going to zoos across the world so that some animals will be in places that are safe from the volcanoes, fires, and earthquakes of their native islands.

In Chinese legends the dragon is thought to bring good luck. Maybe they have saved enough for themselves.

Dragon Facts

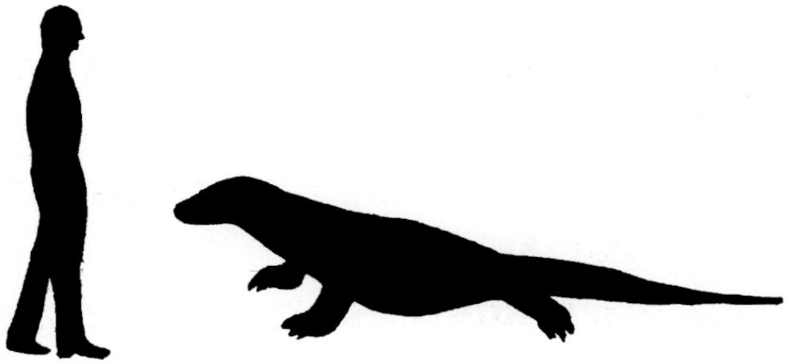

Common Name: Komodo dragon, ora
Babies are called hatchlings or pups. No special name for males or females. No special name for groups.

Scientific Name: *Varanus komodoensis*

Size: Up to ten feet long. Up to 400 pounds after a good meal. Males and females are about the same size, although the biggest dragons are usually male.

Color: Young are greenish black and white with gold speckles, reddish circles, and alternating bands of dark and light stripes on the tail. Adults are a dull gray or earth-tone brown.

Behavior: Solitary, savage

Range/Habitat: Komodo, Rinja, Padar, and Flores: four Indonesian islands that form a barrier between the Pacific Ocean and the Indian Ocean. Wide variety of habitats including rain forest, grassland, seasonal forest, and seashore.

Food: Meat, including carrion. Young dragons eat primarily insects.

Life span: Thought to be as long as fifty years

Incubation time: Eight and a half months until hatching

Predators: Humans, other dragons

Population: Thought to be between 3,000 and 5,000 dragons on all the islands combined. That, however, is only an educated guess. Listed as "rare" on the Endangered Species List.

Index

(Entries in italics refer to photos and captions.)